RECORDED VERSIONS GUITAR

AUTHENTIC TRANSCRIPTIONS WITH NOTES AND TABLATURE

the goo goo dolls
gutterflower

CONTENTS

Music transcriptions by Pete Billmann

ISBN 0-634-04946-1

HAL•LEONARD® CORPORATION

7777 W. BLUEMOUND RD. P.O. BOX 13819 MILWAUKEE, WI 53213

Visit Hal Leonard Online at
www.halleonard.com

In Australia Contact:
Hal Leonard Australia Pty. Ltd.
22 Taunton Drive P.O. Box 5130
Cheltenham East, 3192 Victoria, Australia
Email: ausadmin@halleonard.com

Big Machine

Words and Music by John Rzeznik

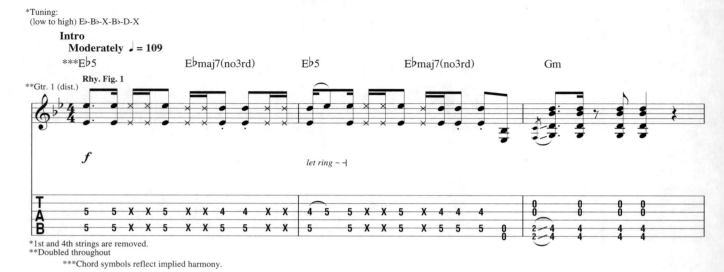

*Tuning:
(low to high) Eb-Bb-X-Bb-D-X

*1st and 4th strings are removed.
**Doubled throughout
***Chord symbols reflect implied harmony.

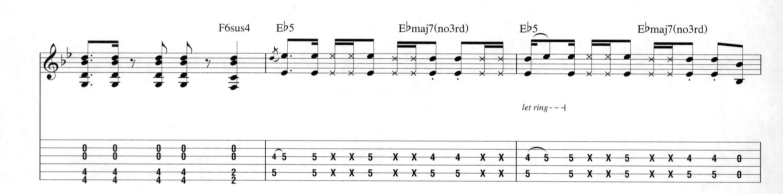

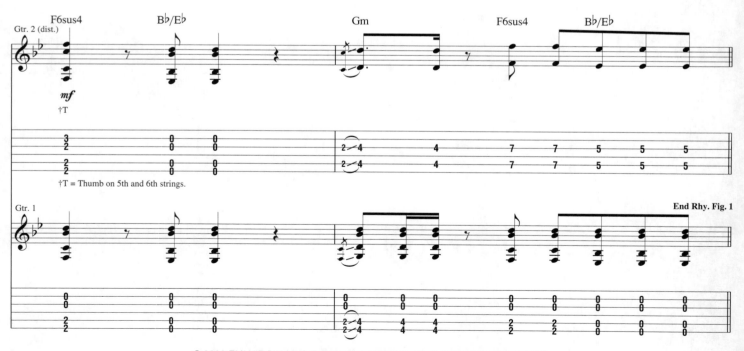

†T = Thumb on 5th and 6th strings.

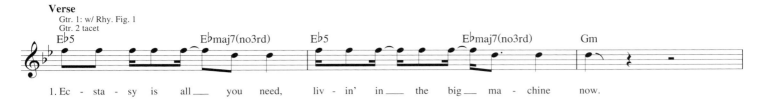

1. Ec - sta - sy is all ___ you need, liv - in' in ___ the big ___ ma - chine now.

Oh, you're so ___ vain. Now your world ___ is way too fast. Noth - in's real ___ and noth - in' lasts and

I'm a - ware. I'm in love, ___ but you don't care.

Turn your an - ger in - to lust. I'm still here, but you don't trust at all. ___ And

F6sus4   Bb/Eb

I'll   be wait - ing. Love and sex and lone - li - ness,__ take what's yours and leave the rest__ so

End Riff A

let ring

let ring

Gtr. 2 tacet

F5   Eb5   Gm   Fsus4   Eb5

I'll   sur - vive.   God,   it's   good   to   be   a - live.__

Gtr. 1

End Rhy. Fig. 2

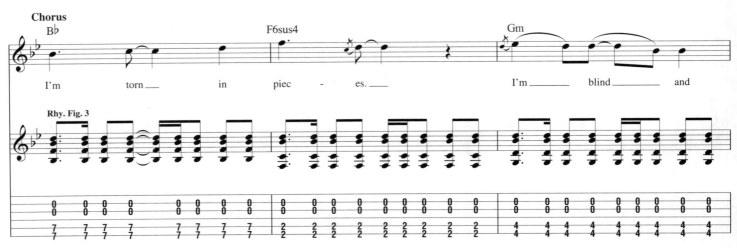

Chorus

Bb   F6sus4   Gm

I'm   torn__   in   piec - es.__   I'm_____ blind_____ and

Rhy. Fig. 3

Interlude

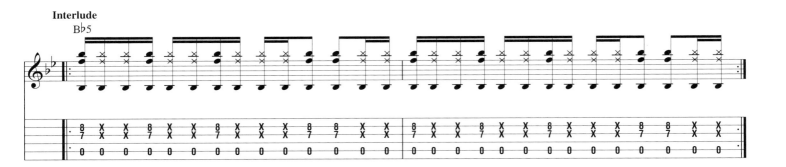

Outro

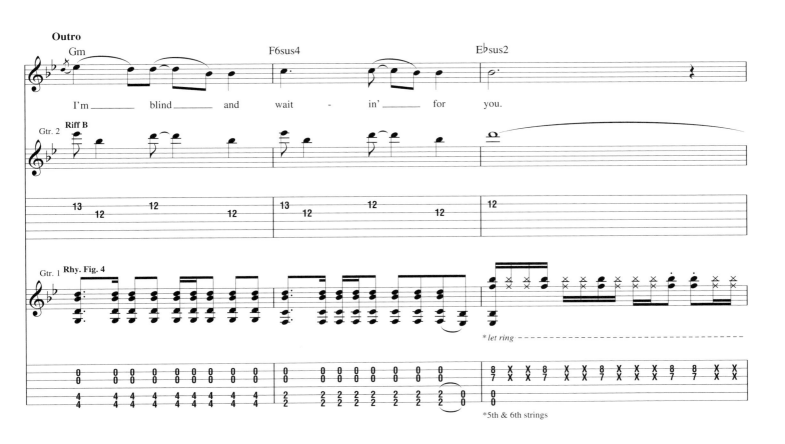

I'm _____ blind _____ and wait - in' _____ for you.

let ring -

*5th & 6th strings

Gtrs. 1 & 2: w/ Rhy. Fig. 4 & Riff B (2 times)

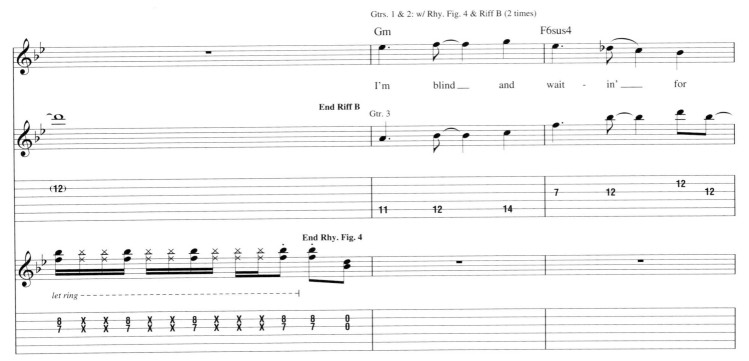

I'm blind ___ and wait - in' ___ for

let ring -

7

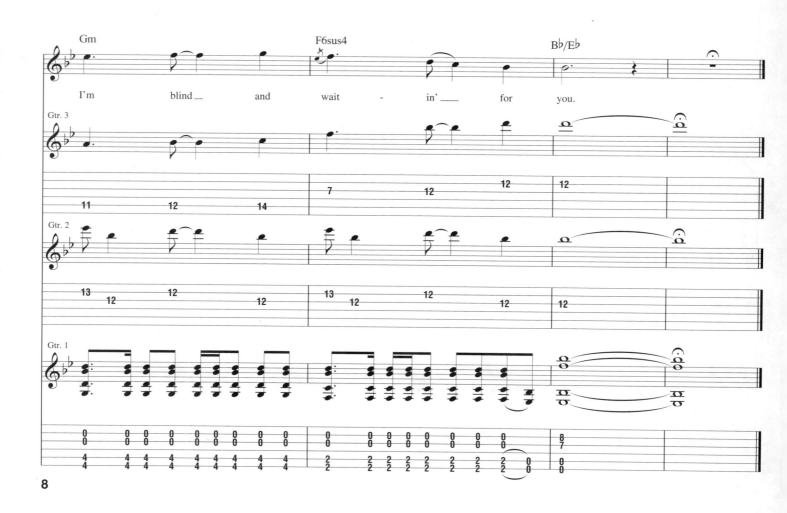

Think About Me

Words and Music by John Rzeznik

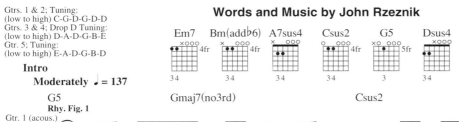

Gtrs. 1 & 2; Tuning:
(low to high) C-G-D-G-D-D
Gtrs. 3 & 4; Drop D Tuning:
(low to high) D-A-D-G-B-E
Gtr. 5; Tuning:
(low to high) E-A-D-G-B-D

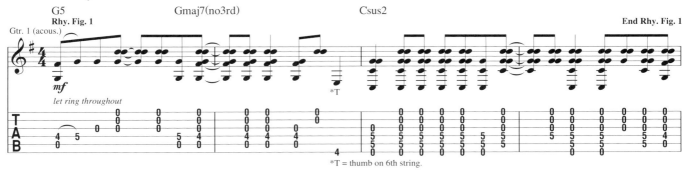

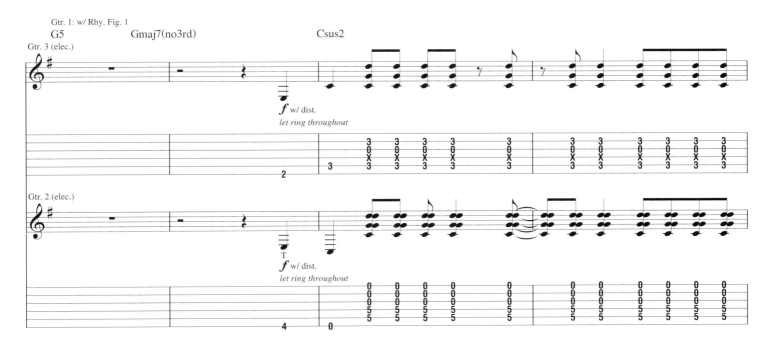

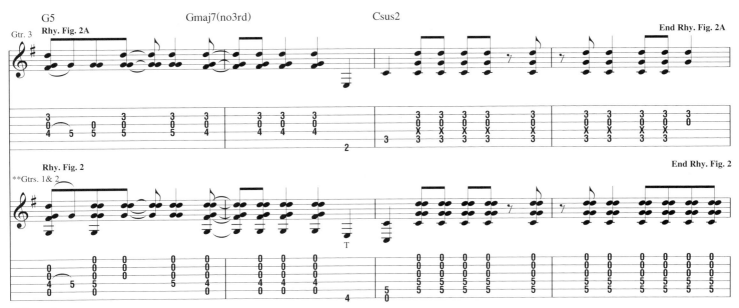

**Composite arrangement

Chorus
Gtrs. 1, 2 & 3: w/ Rhy. Figs. 2 & 2A (2 times)

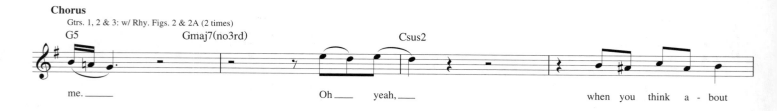

me._____ Oh____ yeah,____ when you think a - bout

me,_____ think a - bout me._____

Verse
Gtrs. 1 & 2: w/ Rhy. Fig. 3 (2 times)

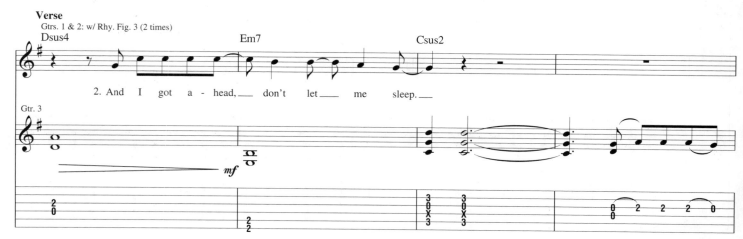

2. And I got a - head,___ don't let___ me sleep.___

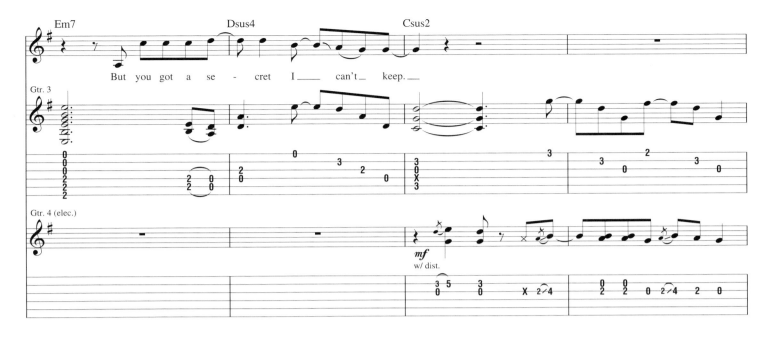

But you got a se - cret I___ can't___ keep.___

Gtr. 3

Gtr. 4 (elec.)

mf
w/ dist.

You see a lit - tle stran - ger in___ your mir - ror.___

let ring

Gtr. 4 tacet

The girl you nev - er knew is what___ you___ fear.___ Oh,

p

Pre-Chorus

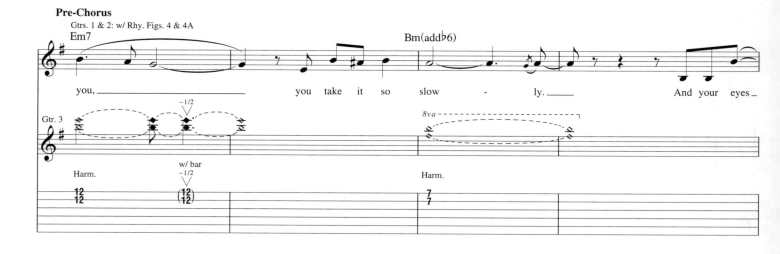

you,_____ you take it so slow - ly.____ And your eyes_

look so lone - ly,____ but it's on-

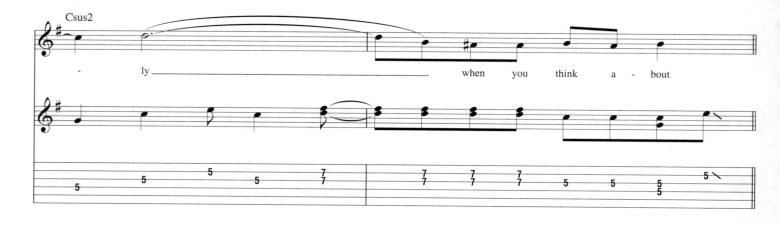

- ly when you think a - bout

Chorus

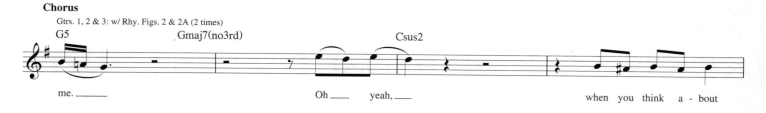

me.____ Oh___ yeah,___ when you think a - bout

me,____ think a - bout me.____ And

Interlude

G5

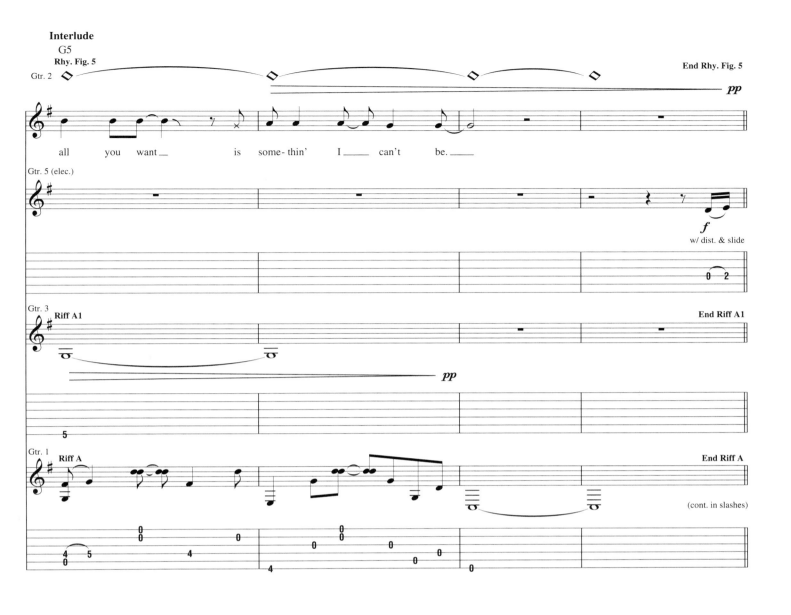

all you want___ is some-thin' I___ can't be.___

Guitar Solo

15

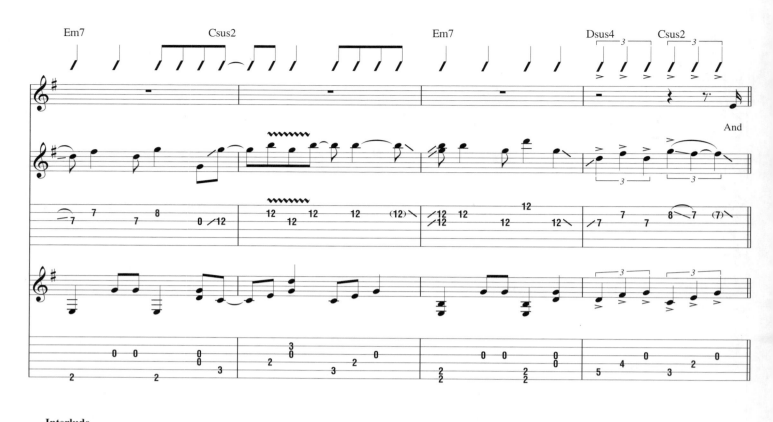

Interlude
Gtrs. 1 & 3: w/ Riffs A & A1
Gtr. 2: w/ Rhy. Fig. 5

all you want___ from me___ is what___ you need. And I'm say - in, now,

Gtr. 5

pp

Pre-Chorus
Gtrs. 1 & 2: w/ Rhy. Figs. 4 & 4A

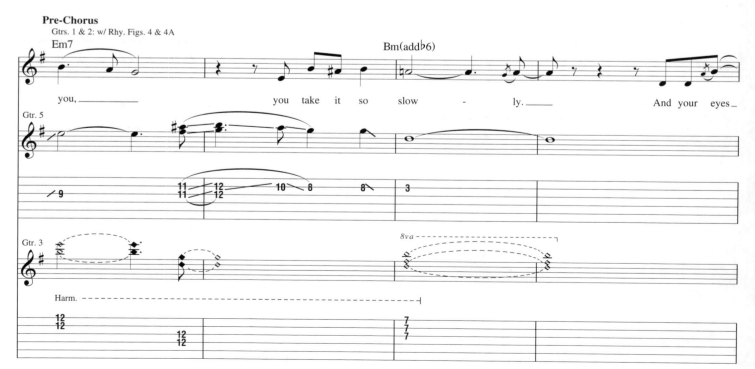

you,___ you take it so slow - ly.___ And your eyes___

Gtr. 5

Gtr. 3

Harm.

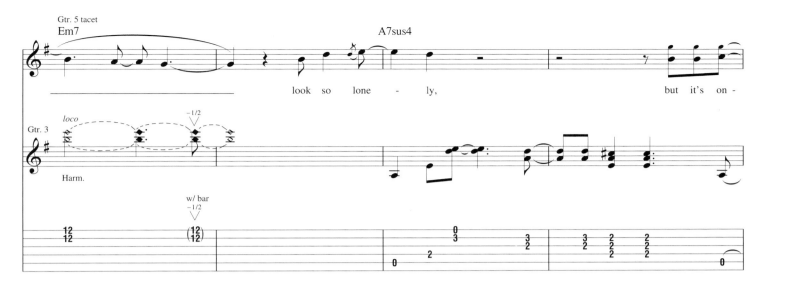

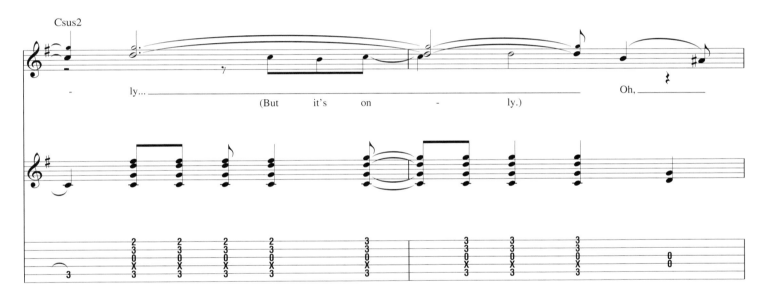

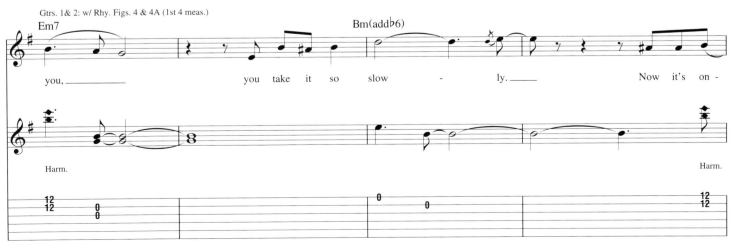

Gtrs. 1 & 2: w/ Rhy. Figs. 4 & 4A (last 4 meas.)

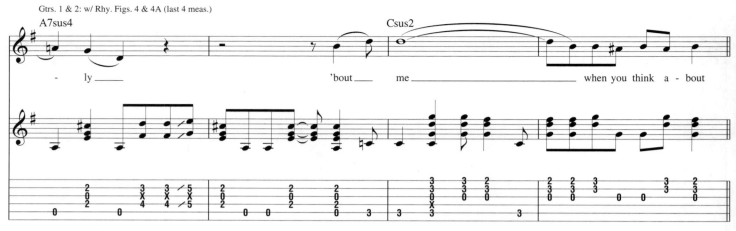

-ly ____ 'bout ____ me _____ when you think a - bout

Outro Chorus

Gtrs. 1, 2 & 3: w/ Rhy. Fig. 2 & 2A (3 times)

me, _____ you think a - bout me. ____ Oh, ____ when you think a - bout

me. _____ Oh ____ yeah, _____ when you think a - bout

me, _____ think a - bout me. _____ Yeah, when you think a - bout
(Oh, ____ yeah.) _____

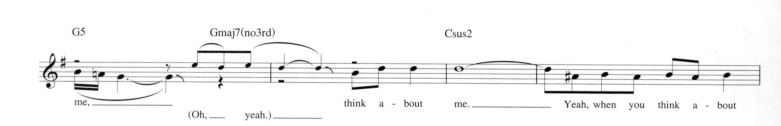

me. _____

Gtr. 3

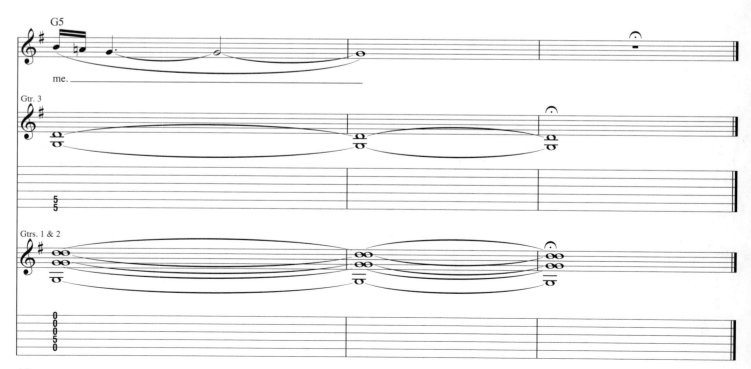

Gtrs. 1 & 2

Here Is Gone

Words and Music by John Rzeznik

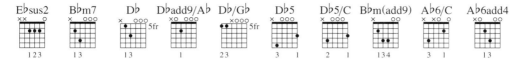

Open Db Tuning:
(low to high) Db-Ab-Db-Ab-Db-F

Intro

Moderately ♩ = 102

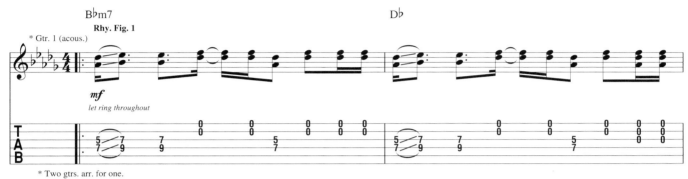

* Two gtrs. arr. for one.

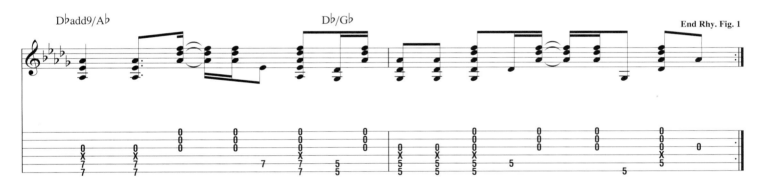

Verse

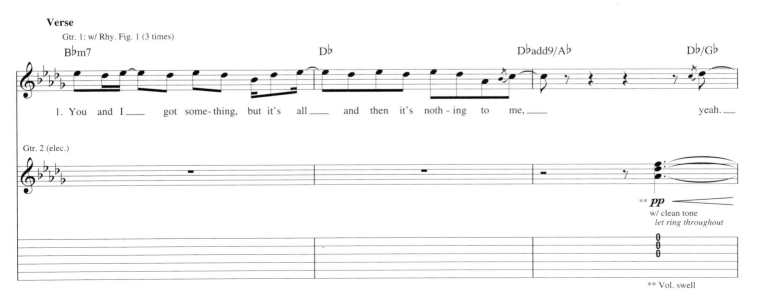

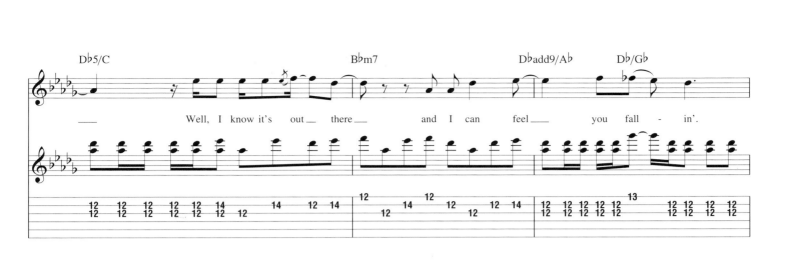

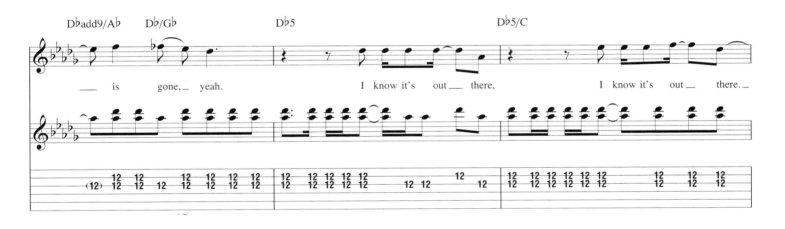

You Never Know

Words and Music by Robbie Takac

*Chord symbols reflect implied harmony.

**Chord symbols implied by Gtr. 3

hit me like___ I nev - er felt___ be - fore.   Sil - ly   for ___   the last___

time._____

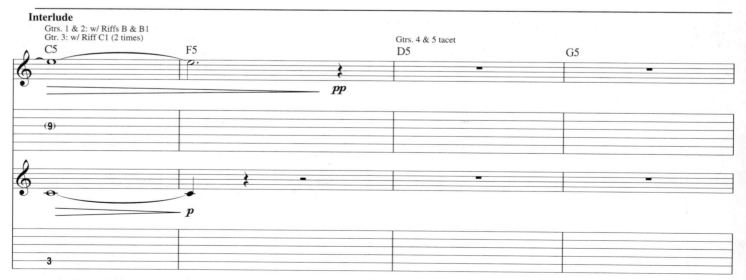

Interlude
Gtrs. 1 & 2: w/ Riffs B & B1
Gtr. 3: w/ Riff C1 (2 times)

Gtrs. 4 & 5 tacet

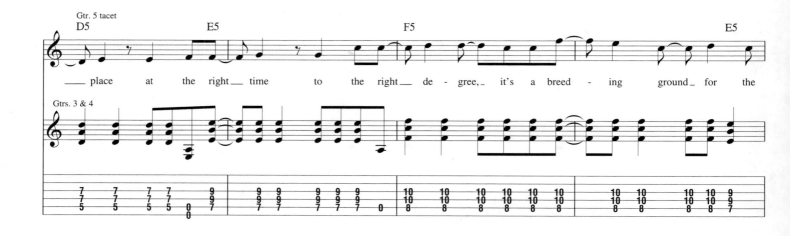

place at the right time to the right de-gree,_ it's a breed - ing ground_ for the

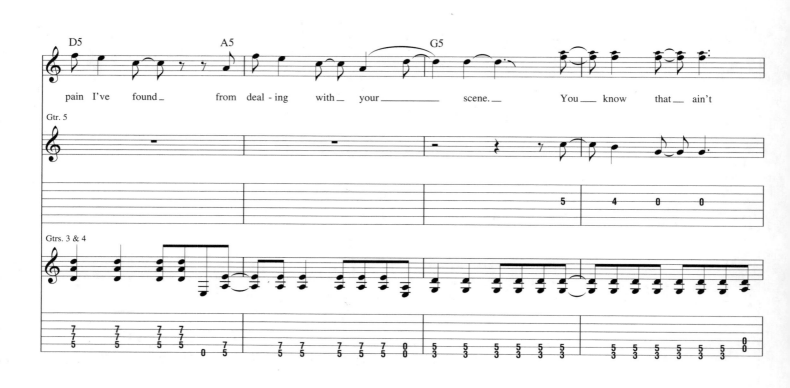

pain I've found_ from deal-ing with_ your _____ scene._ You_ know that_ ain't

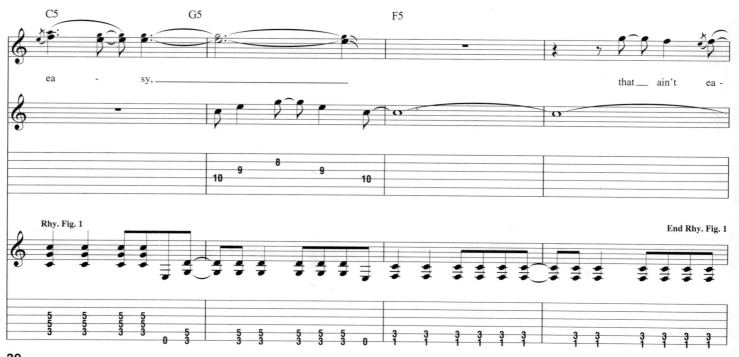

ea - sy, _____ that_ ain't ea-

What a Scene

Words and Music by John Rzeznik

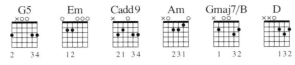

*Harmonic & open strings sound simultaneously.

**Doubled throughout

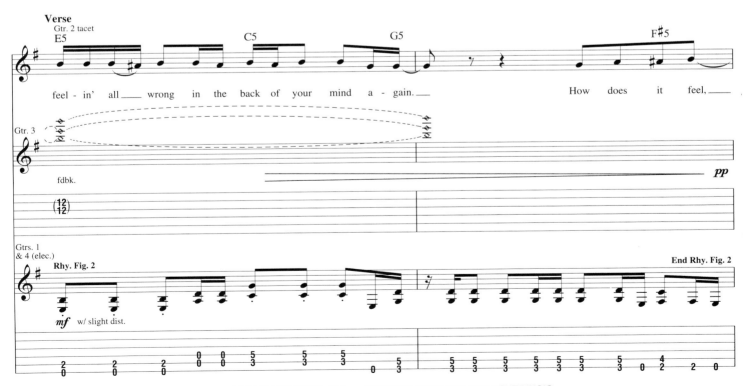

34

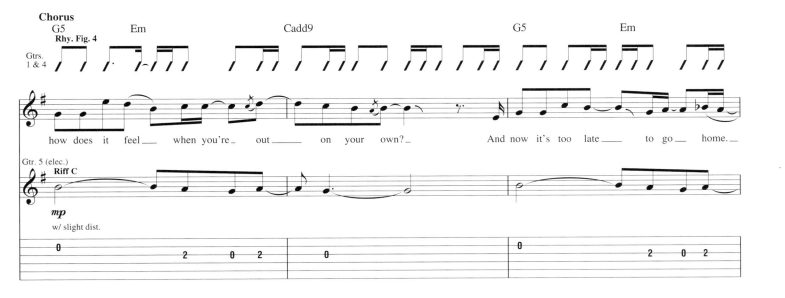

Chorus

how does it feel ___ when you're ___ out ___ on your own? ___ And now it's too late ___ to go ___ home. ___

w/ slight dist.

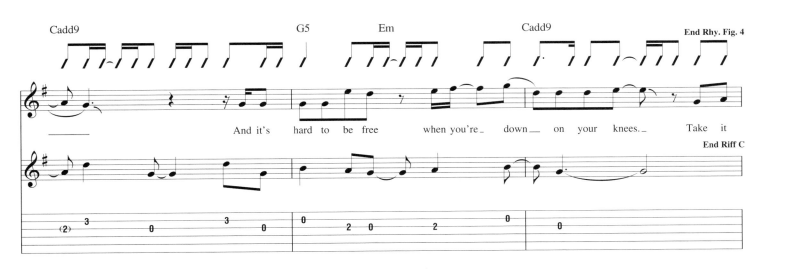

And it's hard to be free when you're ___ down ___ on your knees. ___ Take it

Interlude

Gtrs. 1 & 2: w/ Rhy. Fig. 1 & Riff A
Gtr. 4 tacet   Gtr. 5 tacet

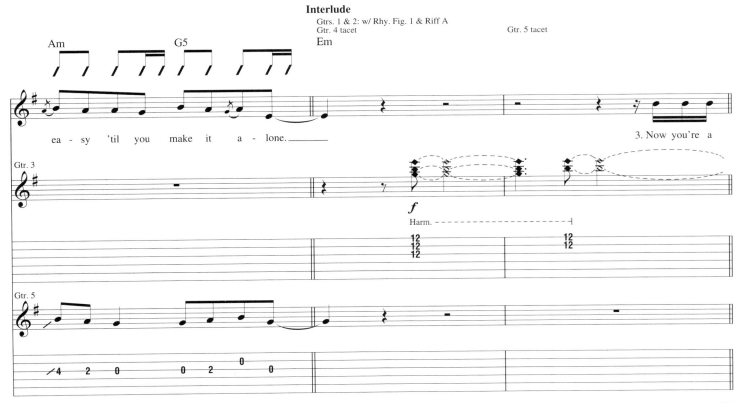

ea-sy 'til you make it a-lone. ___   3. Now you're a

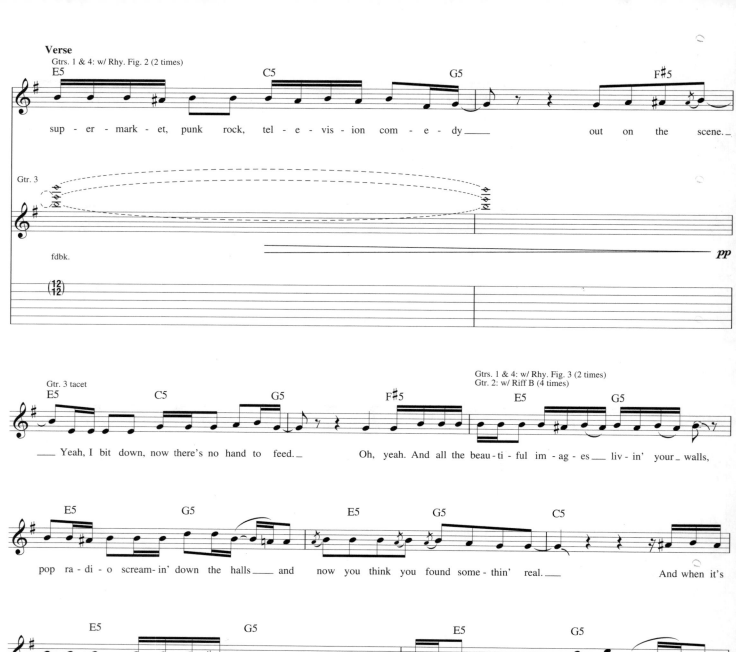

Verse
Gtrs. 1 & 4: w/ Rhy. Fig. 2 (2 times)

E5 C5 G5 F#5

su - per - mark - et, punk rock, tel - e - vis - ion com - e - dy _____ out on the scene. _

Gtr. 3

fdbk. *pp*

(12/12)

Gtr. 3 tacet

Gtrs. 1 & 4: w/ Rhy. Fig. 3 (2 times)
Gtr. 2: w/ Riff B (4 times)

E5 C5 G5 F#5 E5 G5

_____ Yeah, I bit down, now there's no hand to feed. _ Oh, yeah. And all the beau - ti - ful im - ag - es ___ liv - in' your _ walls,

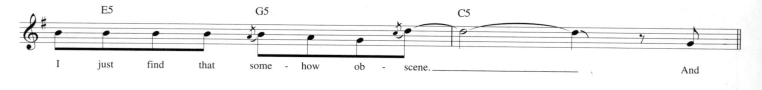

E5 G5 E5 G5 C5

pop ra - di - o scream - in' down the halls ___ and now you think you found some - thin' real. ___ And when it's

E5 G5 E5 G5

all a - bout mon - ey and the things that you need, live a big lie and they all be - lieve. _____ Now,

E5 G5 C5

I just find that some - how ob - scene. _____ And

Chorus
Gtrs. 1, 4 & 5: w/ Rhy. Fig. 4 & Riff C

G5 Em Cadd9 G5 Em

how does it feel ___ to be ___ out ___ on your own? _ And now it's too late ___ to go ___ home.

Cadd9 G5 Em Cadd9

_____ And it's hard to be free when you're _ down ___ on your knees. Take it

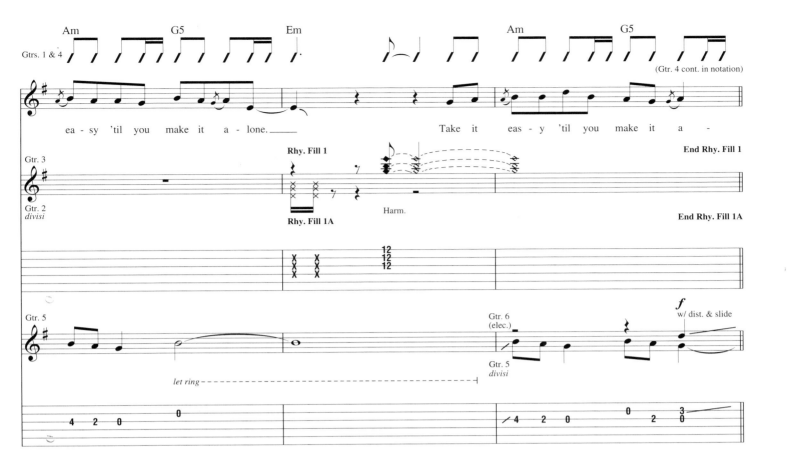

ea - sy 'til you make it a - lone._____ Take it eas - y 'til you make it a -

Rhy. Fill 1   End Rhy. Fill 1

Rhy. Fill 1A   Harm.   End Rhy. Fill 1A

Gtr. 3

Gtr. 2 *divisi*

Gtr. 5

Gtr. 6 (elec.)

Gtr. 5 *divisi*

w/ dist. & slide

let ring

Bridge

lone._____ What a scene,__ yeah.   And it's

Gtrs. 2 & 3 tacet

Gtr. 5 tacet

Cadd9   Gmaj7/B   Em   D   Cadd9

Gtr. 1

Gtr. 6

let ring

Gtr. 4

Gtr. 5

pp

all been_ said_ be - fore and all been_ done._ Take it ea - sy 'til you make it a - lone,

take it eas - y 'til you make it a -

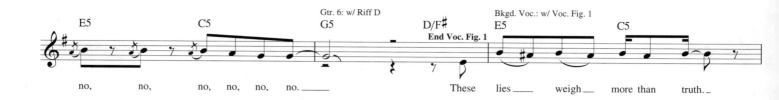

no, no, no, no, no, no. ___ These lies ___ weigh ___ more than truth. ___

In - no - cence ___ looks good on you. ___ Now ev - 'ry - bod - y wants to know ___ your

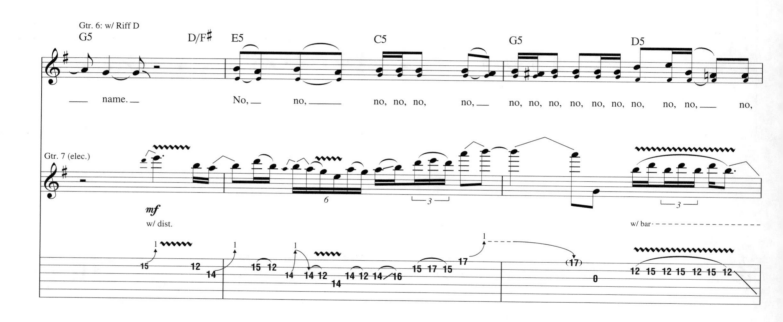

___ name. ___ No, ___ no, ___ no, no, no, no, ___ no, no, no, no, no, no, no, no, ___ no,

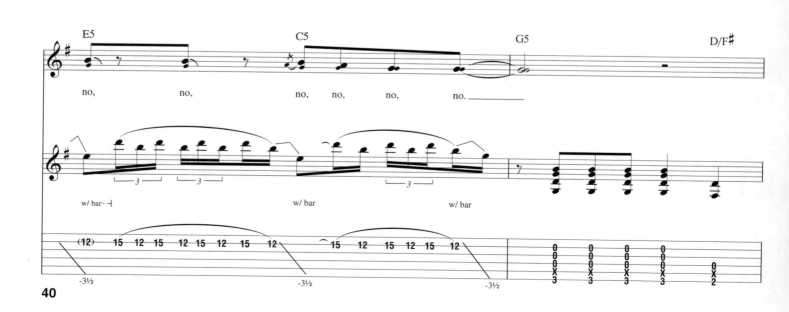

no, no, no, no, no. _____

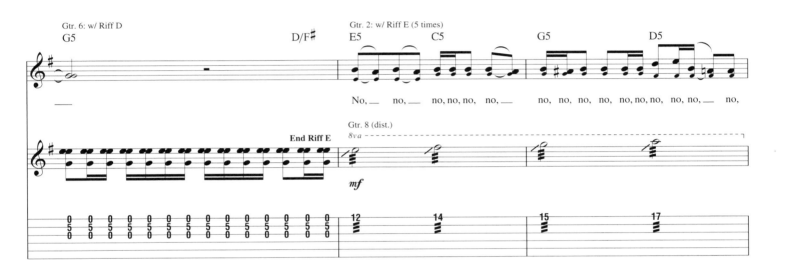

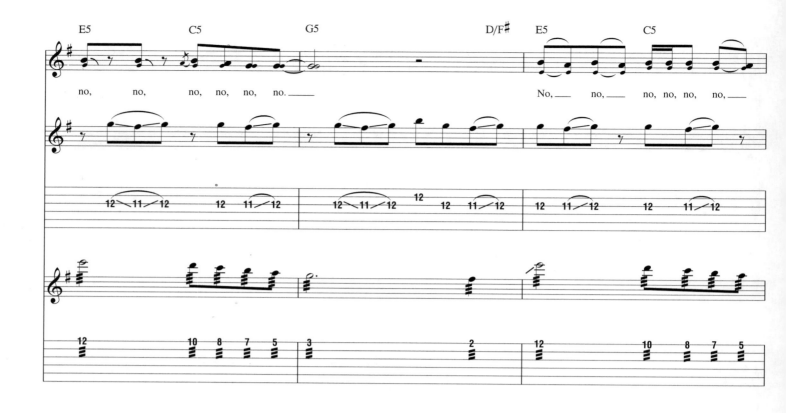

no,   no,   no, no, no, no. _____   No, ___   no, ___   no, no, no,   no, ___

no, no, no, no, no, no, no, no, no, ___ ___ no,   no,   no,   no, no, no, no. _____

Up, Up, Up

Words and Music by Robbie Takac

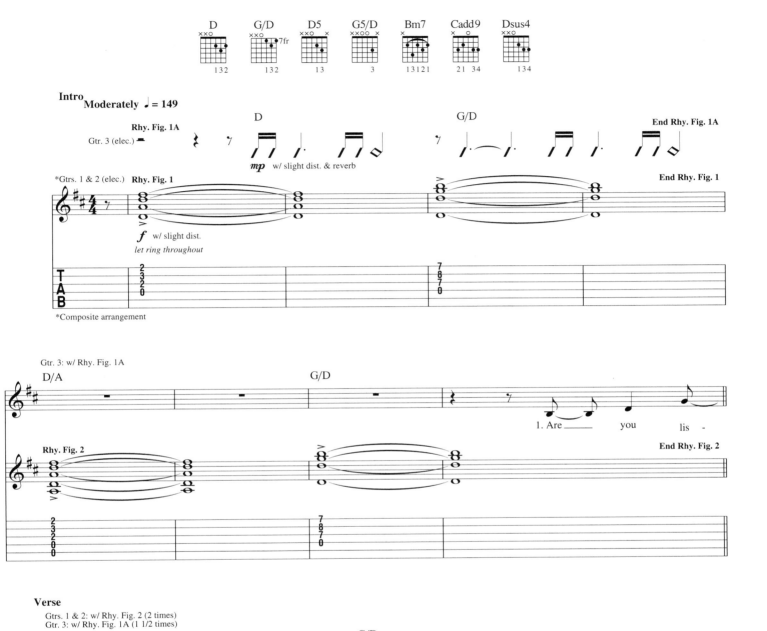

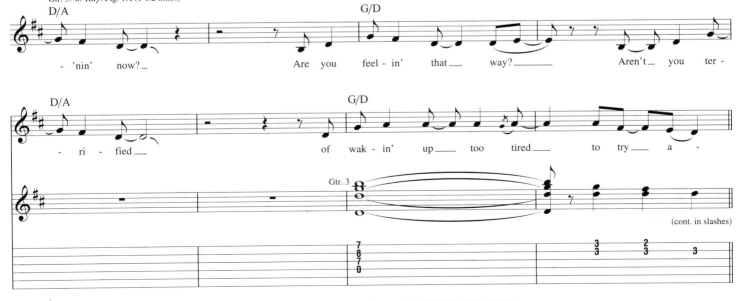

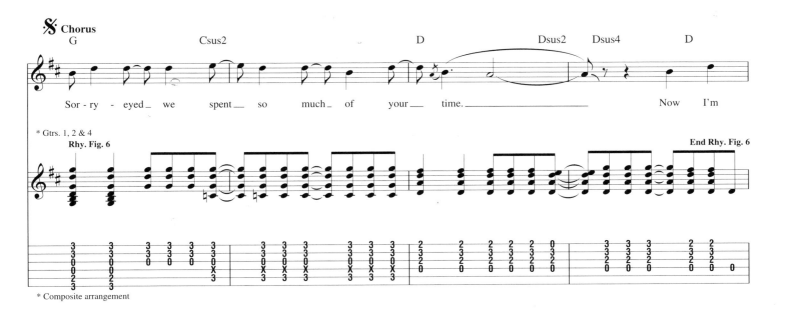

Sor - ry - eyed we spent so much of your time. Now I'm

try'n' to put your rid - dle to a rhyme. And it's up,

up, up; I'm head - in' for this eve - nin'. And it's up,

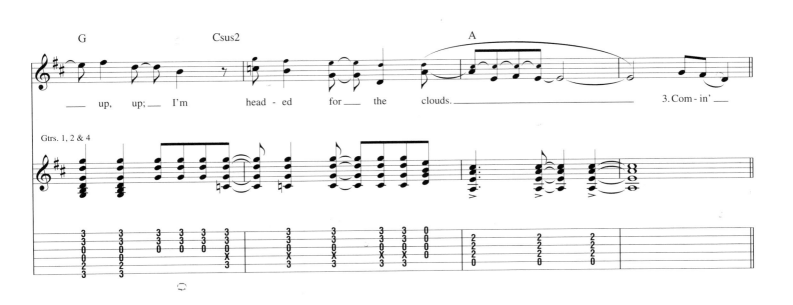

up, up; I'm head - ed for the clouds. 3.Com - in'

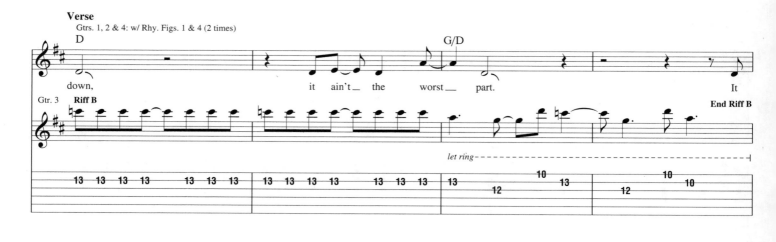

It's Over

Words and Music by John Rzeznik

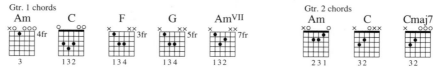

Gtr. 1: Tuning:
(low to high) C-A-C-E-C-E

Intro

Moderately ♩ = 96

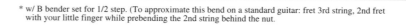

* w/ B bender set for 1/2 step. (To approximate this bend on a standard guitar: fret 3rd string, 2nd fret
with your little finger while prebending the 2nd string behind the nut.

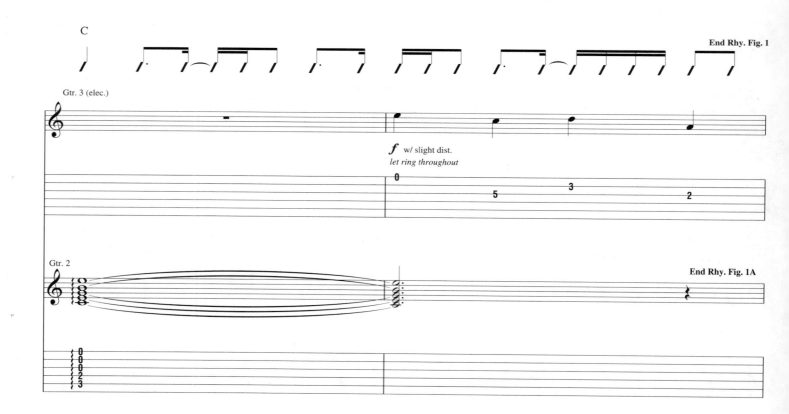

Chord symbols reflect overall harmony.

Verse

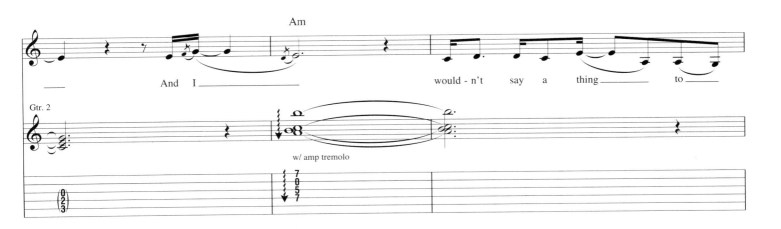

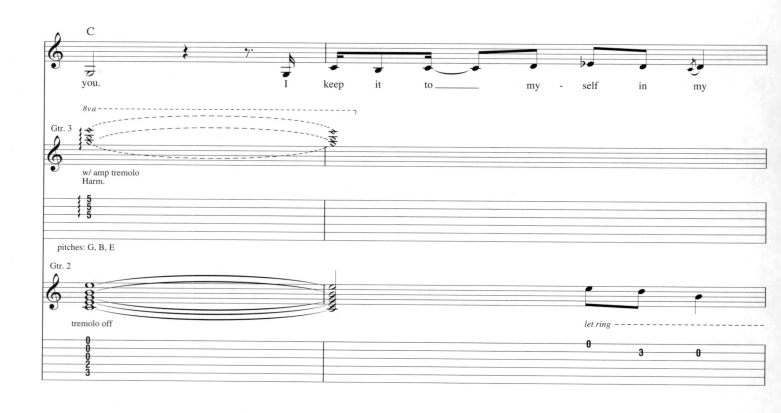

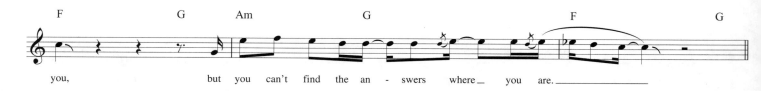

you, but you can't find the an - swers where you are.

Interlude

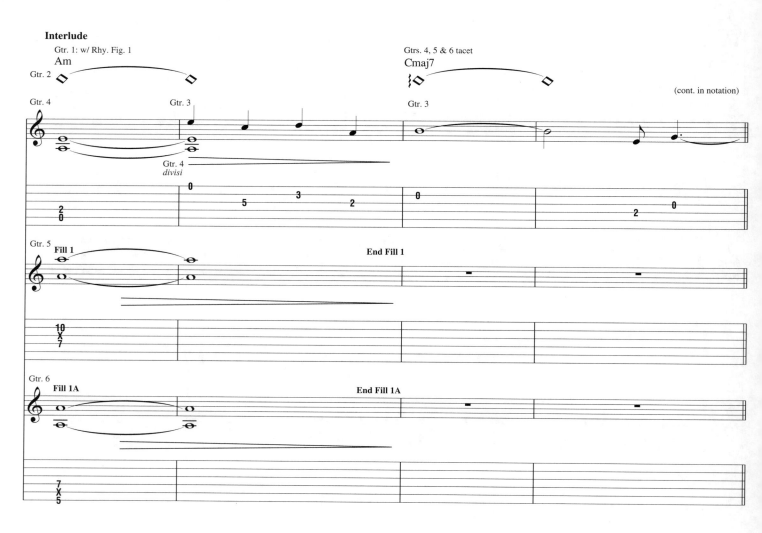

Verse

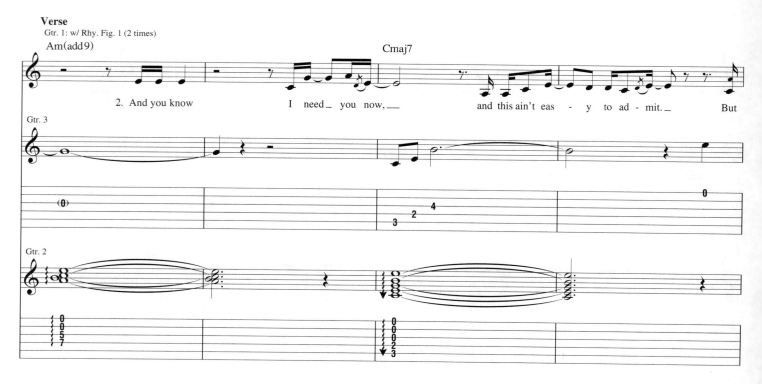

2. And you know I need you now, and this ain't eas - y to ad - mit. But

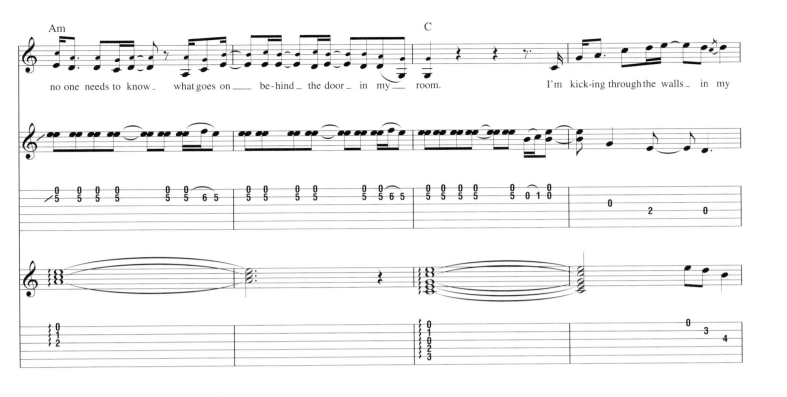

no one needs to know ___ what goes on ___ be-hind ___ the door ___ in my ___ room.   I'm kick-ing through the walls ___ in my

Gtrs. 1 & 4: w/ Rhy. Figs. 2 & 2A
Gtrs. 2 & 3: w/ Riffs A & A1

mind. _____   And   I can't stand with-out ___ you,   and   I won't find the an - swers when ___ you're gone.   But it's

Fill 2
Gtr. 5

End Fill 2

Gtr. 6
divisi

Gtr. 6 to left of slash in tab.

𝄋 **Chorus**
Gtrs. 1 & 4: w/ Rhy. Figs. 3 & 3A (4 times)
Gtrs. 5 & 6: w/ Riffs B & B1 (2 times)
2nd time, Gtrs. 2 & 3 tacet

o - ver ___ to ___ you,   and I can't find the an - swers when ___ you're gone. _____   And it's

To Coda ⊕

o - ver ___ to ___ you,   but you can't find the an - swers where ___ you are. _____

Interlude
Gtrs. 5 & 6: w/ Fills 1 & 1A

Bridge

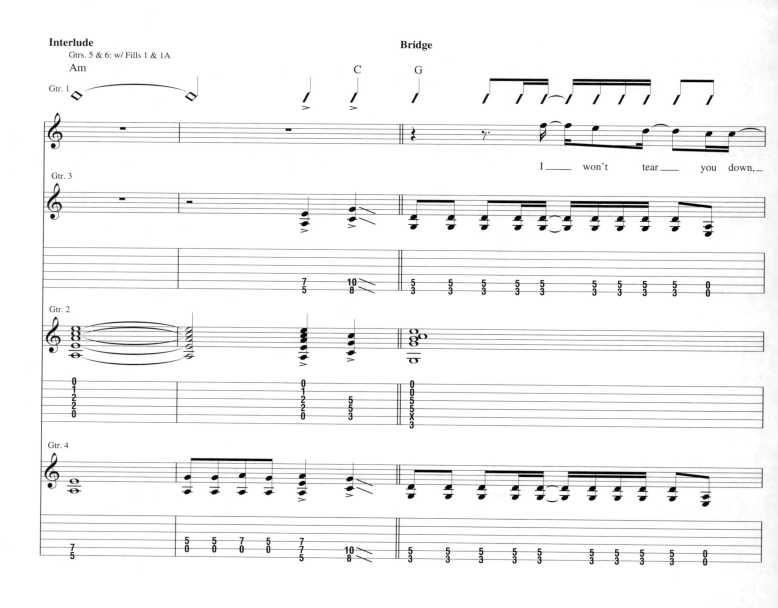

I ____ won't ____ tear ____ you down, ____

I ____ won't tear ____ you down ____ to get in - to ____ the world ____ you want - ed.

*Composite arrangement

Sympathy

Words and Music by John Rzeznik

Chorus

Gtr. 1: w/ Rhy. Fig. 1 (1¾ times)

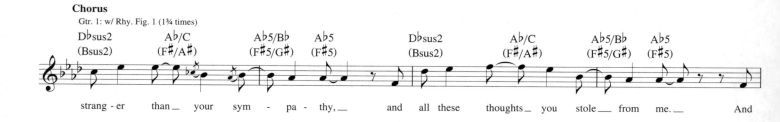

strang - er than __ your sym - pa - thy, __ and all these thoughts __ you stole __ from me. __ And

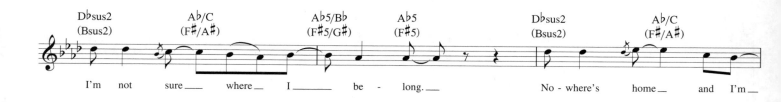

I'm not sure __ where __ I _____ be - long. __ No - where's home __ and I'm

Bridge

__ all wrong. __ And I __ was-n't all __ the things __ I tried __ to make __ be - lieve.

Gtr. 1

__ I __ was. And I __ would-n't be __ the one __ to kneel __ be - fore __ the dreams __

Outro

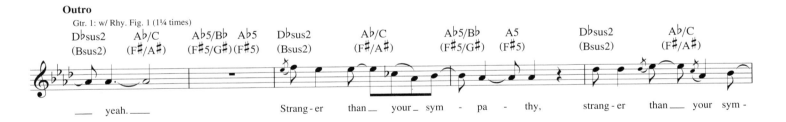

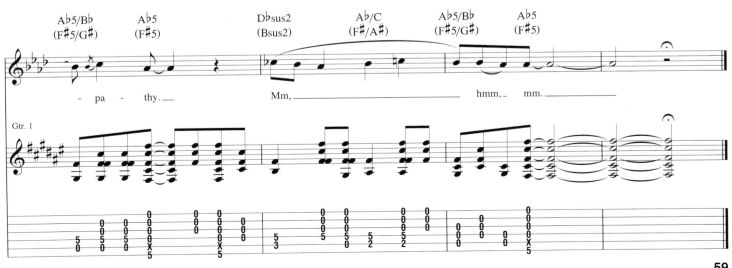

What Do You Need?

Words and Music by John Rzeznik

Tuning:
(low to high) D-G-C-F-A-E

Intro

Moderately ♩ = 112

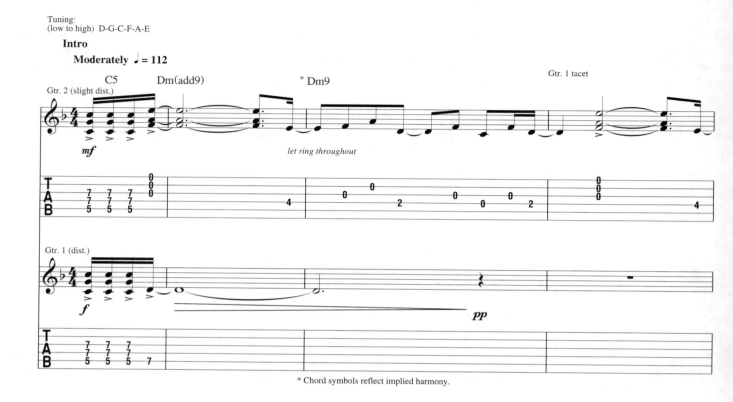

* Chord symbols reflect implied harmony.

Verse

1. What do you need___ from me___ to-night? I feel you look___ right through_ me now.___

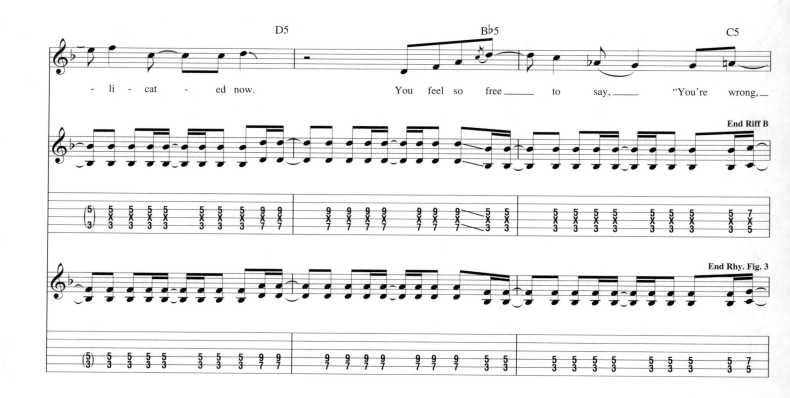

-li - cat - ed now. You feel so free ___ to say, ___ "You're wrong, ___

End Riff B

End Rhy. Fig. 3

___ you're wrong, ___ you're wrong, ___ you're wrong." ___

Interlude

Gtr. 2

Gtr. 3 (clean)

mf

Gtr. 1

let ring

pp

Smash

Words and Music by Robbie Takac

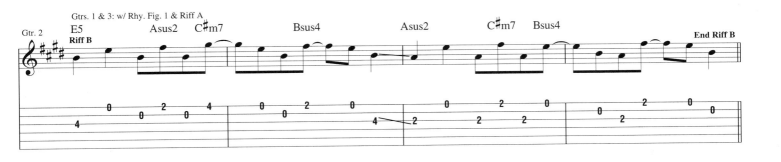

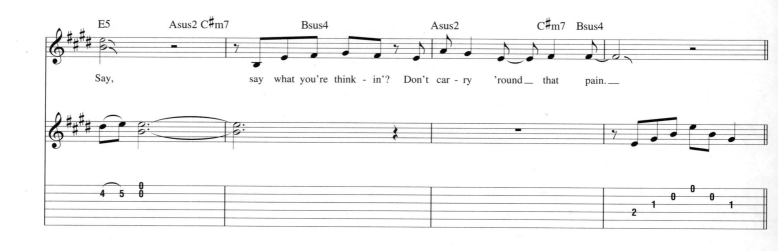

Say, say what you're think - in'? Don't car - ry 'round that pain.

Chorus

Ev - 'ry time I see you pick - in' at your - self, I

Interlude

Gtrs. 1 & 3: w/ Rhy. Fig. 1 & Riff A (2 times)
Gtrs. 4 & 5 tacet

love,   I   love — when   things — work   out.

2. Smash.

I   heard   ya   cry - in'   sev - en   times — this   year. —

com - in' home ___ be - fore I hit ___ the ground. ___

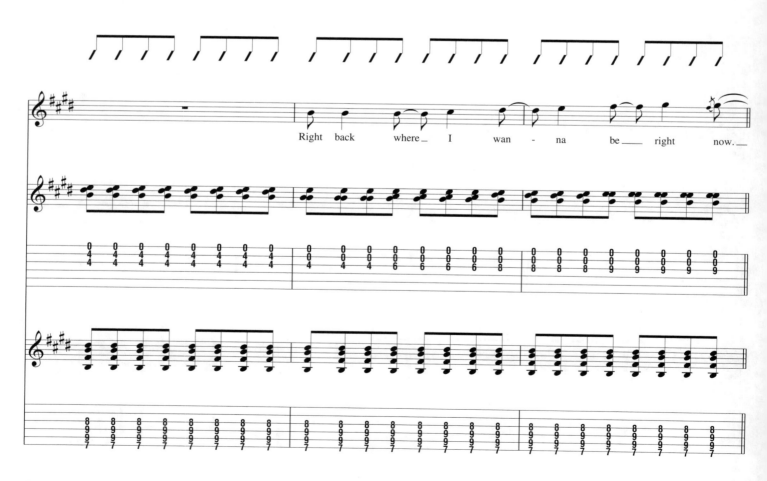

Right back where ___ I wan - na be ___ right now. ___

Tucked Away

Words and Music by Robbie Takac

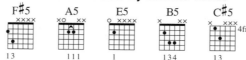

Intro

Moderately Fast ♩ = 175

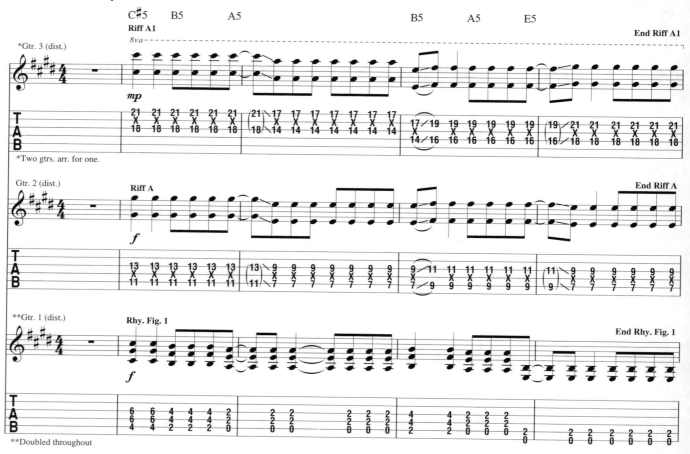

*Two gtrs. arr. for one.

**Doubled throughout

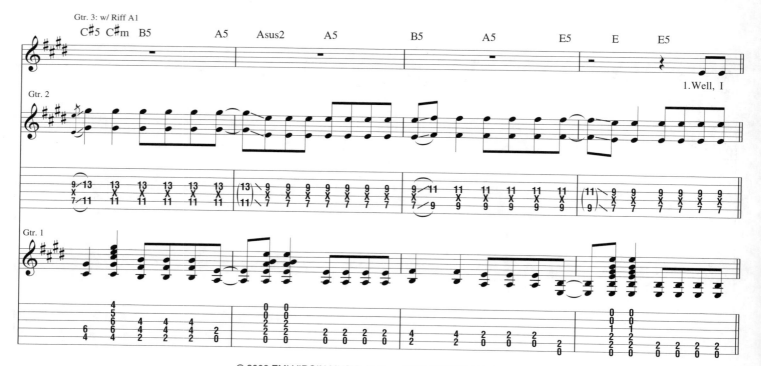

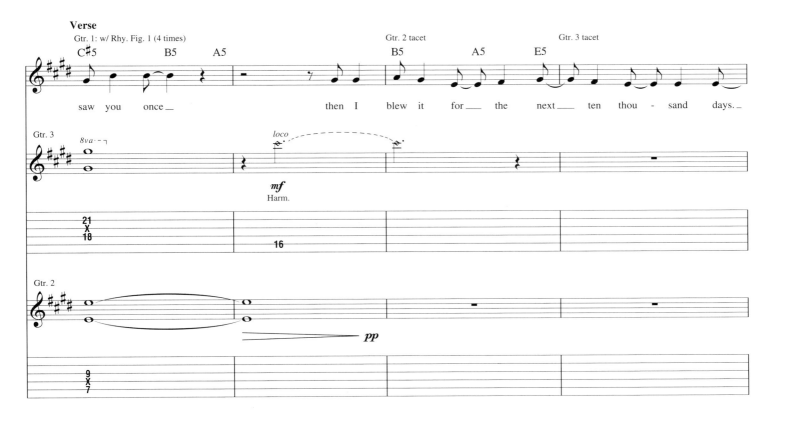

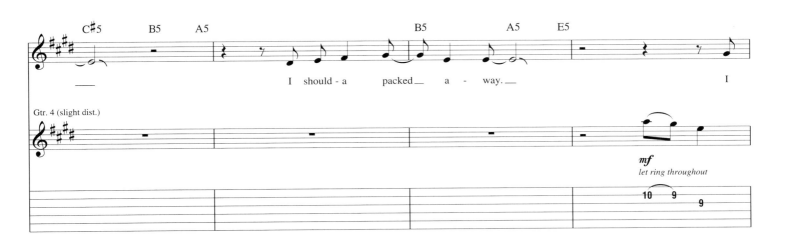

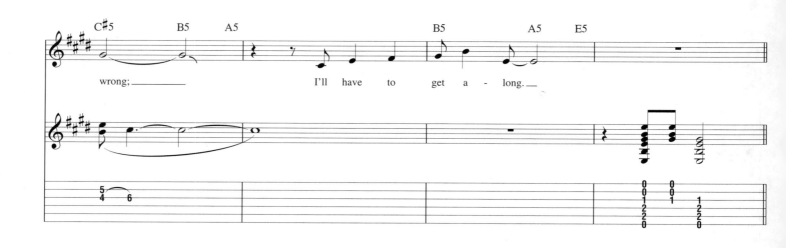

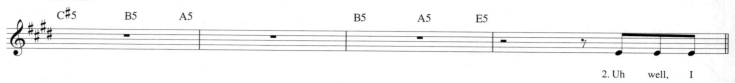

2. Uh well, I

Verse

spent the whole day yes- ter- day on cli- ches a- bout love,

mak- ing me re- mem- ber when your push- es be- come shoves. I

- ter - day, ___ and I'm ___ o - kay. _____ I'll

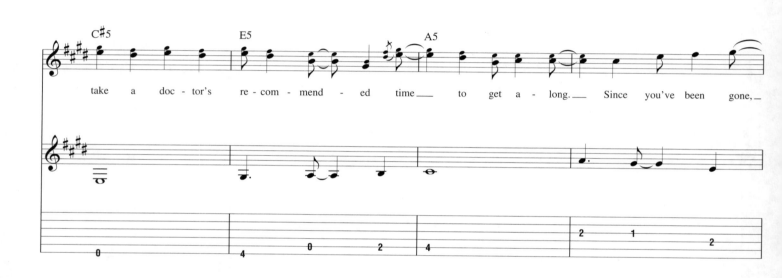

take a doc - tor's re - com - mend - ed time ___ to get a - long. ___ Since you've been gone, ___

Gtr. 1

(cont. in notation)

I'll get a - long, ___ oh, an - y way ___ at all. ___

Guitar Solo

Chorus

Ma - ma just called, said she's tucked a - way.

Truth Is a Whisper

Words and Music by John Rzeznik

Gtrs. 1, 2 & 4: Tuning:
(low to high) C-F-Bb-Eb-C-D

Gtrs. 3 & 5: Tuning:
(low to high) C-F-Bb-G-C-D

Intro

Moderately ♩ = 135

*Cm7

* Chord symbols reflect combined harmony.

Gtrs. 1 & 2: w/ Riffs A & A1

Gtr. 3

Verse

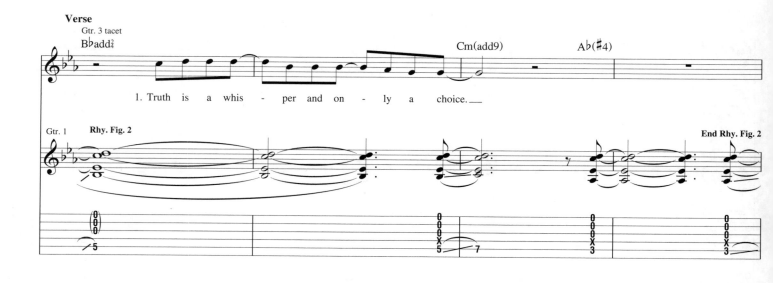

1. Truth is a whis - per and on - ly a choice.___

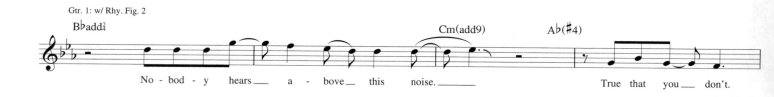

No - bod - y hears___ a - bove___ this noise._____ True that you___ don't.

It's al - ways a risk___ when you try___ to be - lieve,___ on - ly some - times.

I know there's so___ much___ than me,___ yeah._____

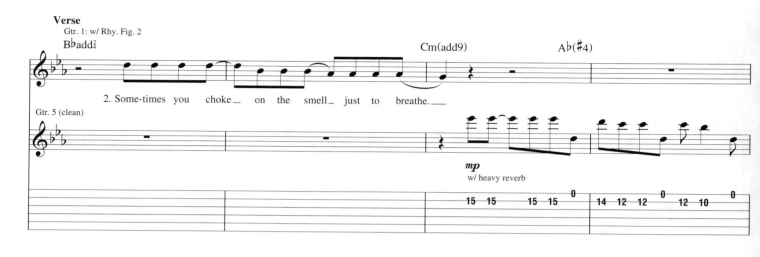

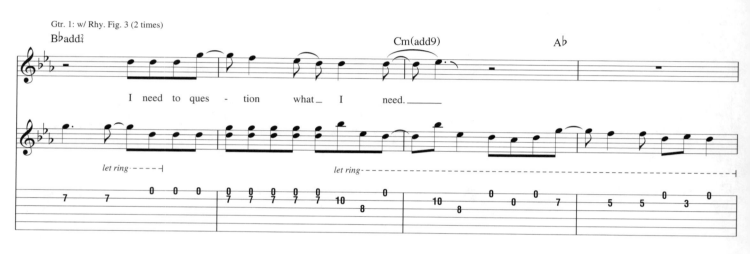

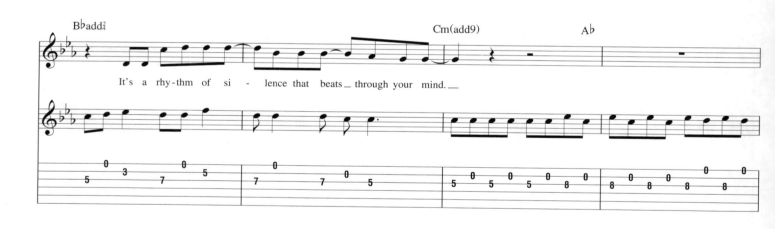

And I got caught in the ruse of the world. It's just a prom - ise no one ev - er keeps.

And now it's chang - ing in your sleep, and no one here can see.

Chorus

Gtr. 1: w/ Rhy. Fig. 1 (1st 7 meas.)
Gtrs. 2 & 4: w/ Riffs B & B1 (2 times)

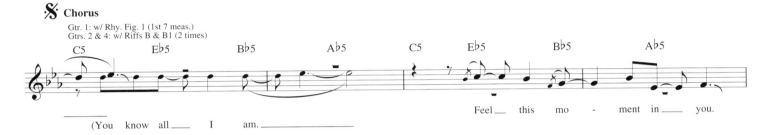

(You know all I am. Feel this mo - ment in you.

To Coda

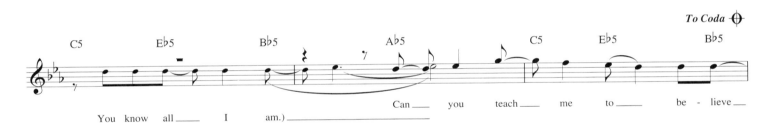

You know all I am.) Can you teach me to be - lieve

Bridge

in some - thing? And who's the one you an - swer to? Do you

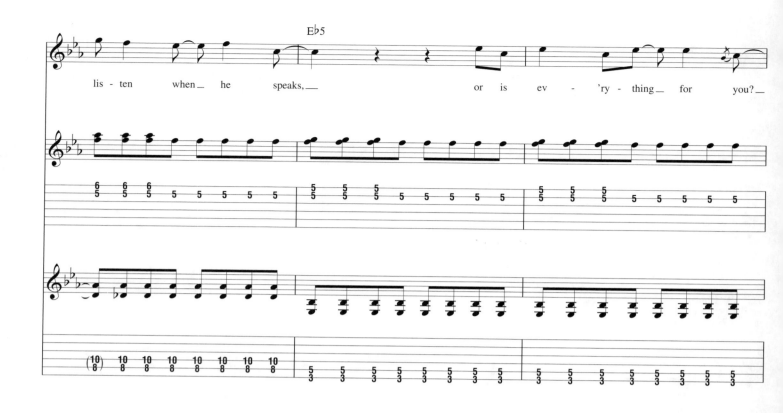

lis - ten   when __ he   speaks, __   or   is   ev - 'ry - thing __ for   you? __

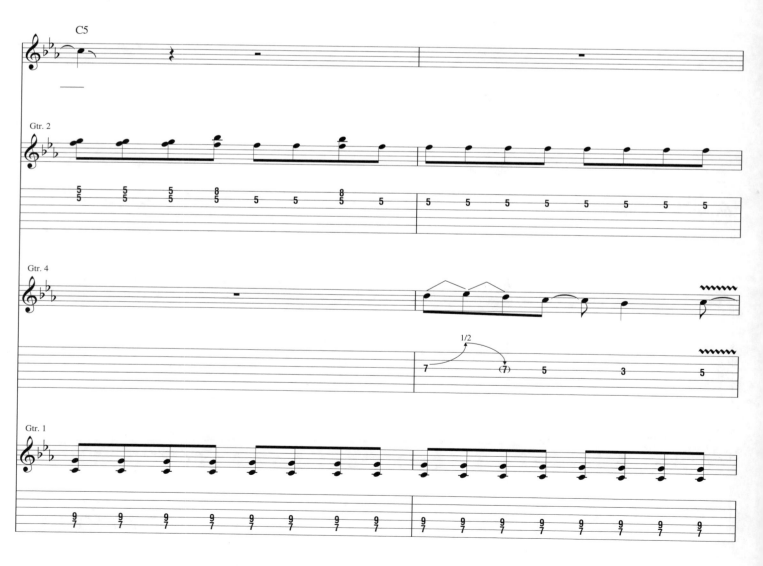

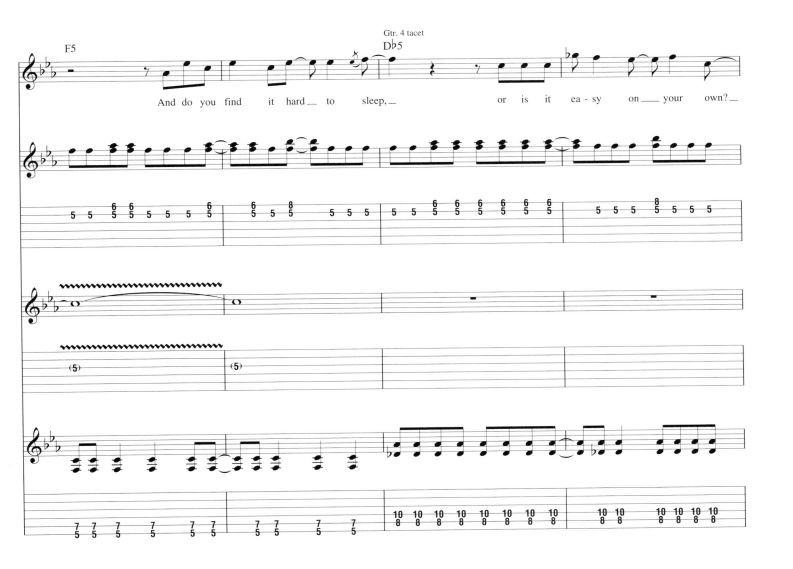

And do you find it hard__ to sleep,__ or is it ea - sy on__ your own?__

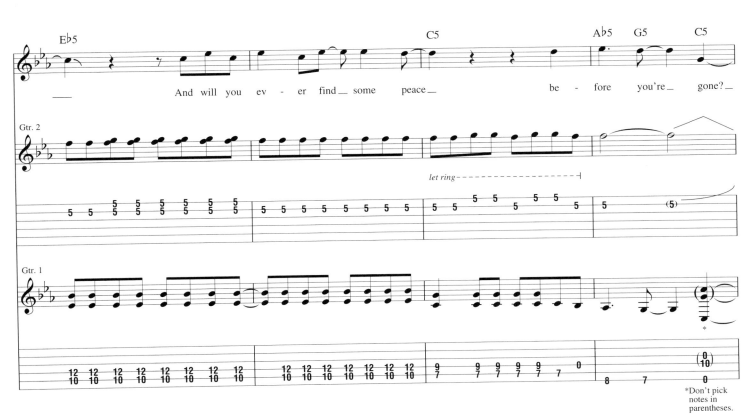

And will you ev - er find__ some peace__ be - fore you're__ gone?__

*Don't pick
notes in
parentheses.

Interlude

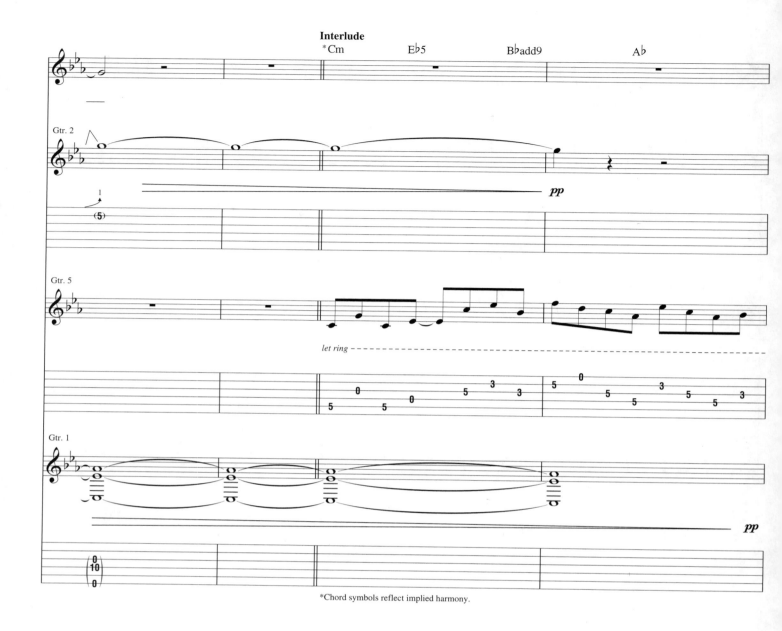

*Chord symbols reflect implied harmony.

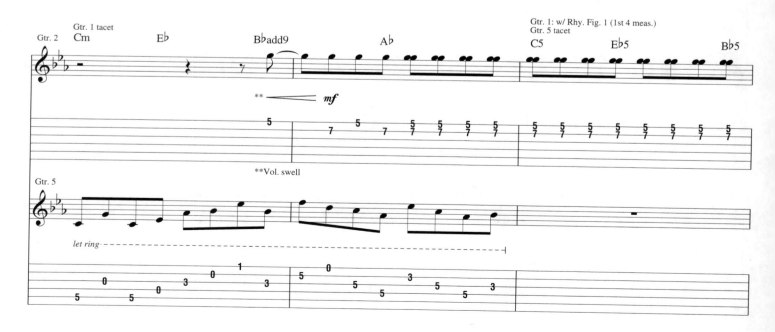

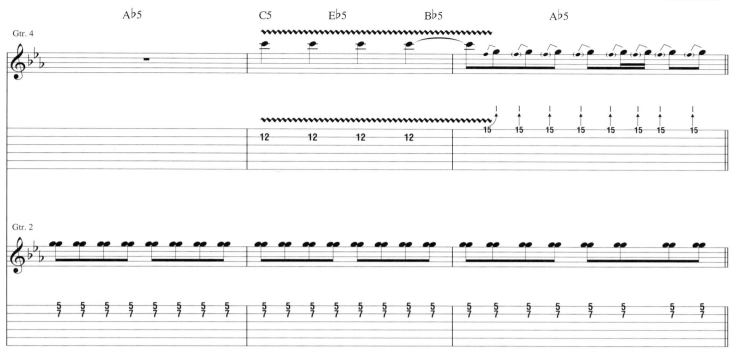

Coda

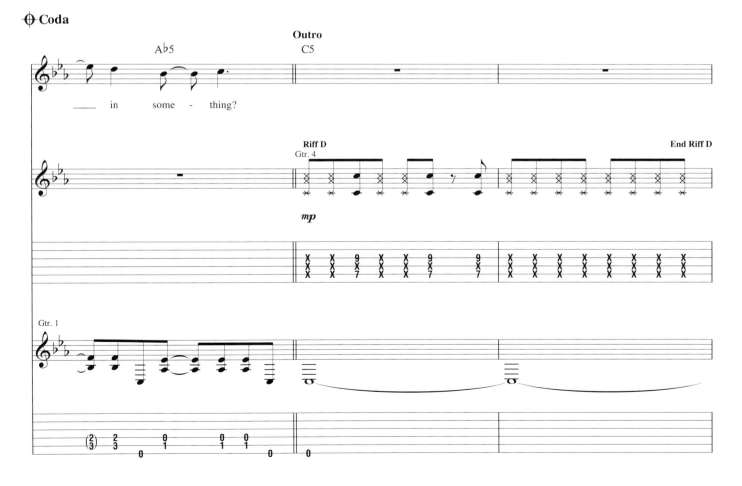

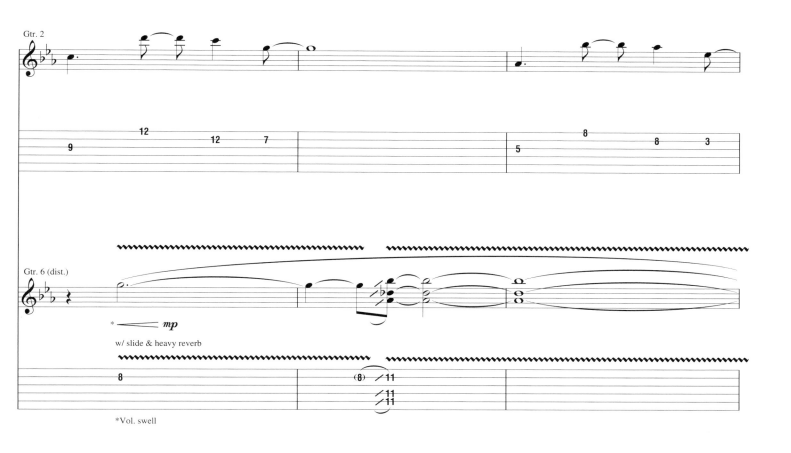

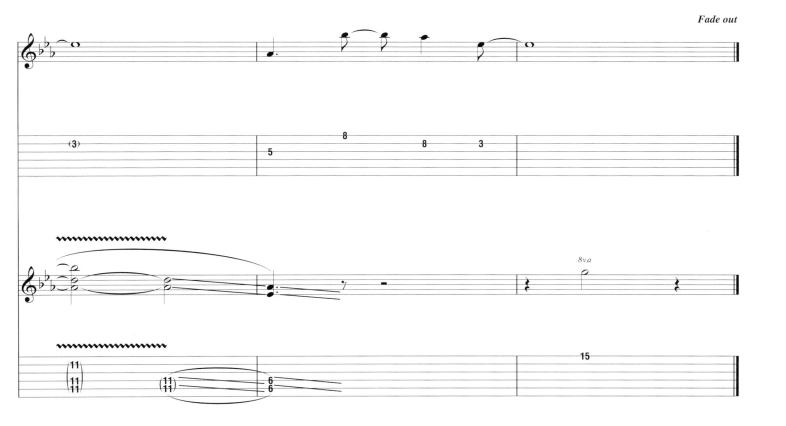

Guitar Notation Legend

Guitar Music can be notated three different ways: on a *musical staff*, in *tablature*, and in *rhythm slashes*.

RHYTHM SLASHES are written above the staff. Strum chords in the rhythm indicated. Use the chord diagrams found at the top of the first page of the transcription for the appropriate chord voicings. Round noteheads indicate single notes.

THE MUSICAL STAFF shows pitches and rhythms and is divided by bar lines into measures. Pitches are named after the first seven letters of the alphabet.

TABLATURE graphically represents the guitar fingerboard. Each horizontal line represents a string, and each number represents a fret.

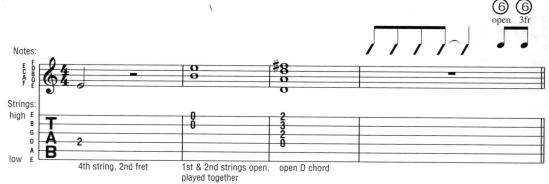

4th string, 2nd fret   1st & 2nd strings open, played together   open D chord

HALF-STEP BEND: Strike the note and bend up 1/2 step.

WHOLE-STEP BEND: Strike the note and bend up one step.

GRACE NOTE BEND: Strike the note and immediately bend up as indicated.

SLIGHT (MICROTONE) BEND: Strike the note and bend up 1/4 step.

BEND AND RELEASE: Strike the note and bend up as indicated, then release back to the original note. Only the first note is struck.

PRE-BEND: Bend the note as indicated, then strike it.

VIBRATO: The string is vibrated by rapidly bending and releasing the note with the fretting hand.

WIDE VIBRATO: The pitch is varied to a greater degree by vibrating with the fretting hand.

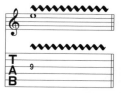

HAMMER-ON: Strike the first (lower) note with one finger, then sound the higher note (on the same string) with another finger by fretting it without picking.

PULL-OFF: Place both fingers on the notes to be sounded. Strike the first note and without picking, pull the finger off to sound the second (lower) note.

LEGATO SLIDE: Strike the first note and then slide the same fret-hand finger up or down to the second note. The second note is not struck.

SHIFT SLIDE: Same as legato slide, except the second note is struck.

TRILL: Very rapidly alternate between the notes indicated by continuously hammering on and pulling off.

TAPPING: Hammer ("tap") the fret indicated with the pick-hand index or middle finger and pull off to the note fretted by the fret hand.

NATURAL HARMONIC: Strike the note while the fret-hand lightly touches the string directly over the fret indicated.

PINCH HARMONIC: The note is fretted normally and a harmonic is produced by adding the edge of the thumb or the tip of the index finger of the pick hand to the normal pick attack.

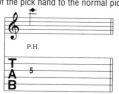

PICK SCRAPE: The edge of the pick is rubbed down (or up) the string, producing a scratchy sound.

MUFFLED STRINGS: A percussive sound is produced by laying the fret hand across the string(s) without depressing, and striking them with the pick hand.

PALM MUTING: The note is partially muted by the pick hand lightly touching the string(s) just before the bridge.

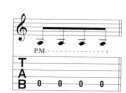

RAKE: Drag the pick across the strings indicated with a single motion.

TREMOLO PICKING: The note is picked as rapidly and continuously as possible.

VIBRATO BAR DIVE AND RETURN: The pitch of the note or chord is dropped a specified number of steps (in rhythm) then returned to the original pitch.

VIBRATO BAR SCOOP: Depress the bar just before striking the note, then quickly release the bar.

VIBRATO BAR DIP: Strike the note and then immediately drop a specified number of steps, then release back to the original pitch.